IMAGES
of Sport

ST JOHNSTONE
FOOTBALL CLUB

A homely, local club: the business entrance to Muirton Park, pictured on the day of the last-ever match played there, in 1989.

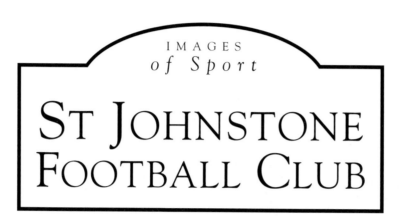

IMAGES
of Sport

ST JOHNSTONE
FOOTBALL CLUB

Alastair Blair

TEMPUS

When it's good, it's brilliant. A young fan celebrates St Johnstone's promotion to the Scottish Premier Division in 1990.

First published 2003

Tempus Publishing Limited
The Mill, Brimscombe Port,
Stroud, Gloucestershire, GL5 2QG

British Library Cataloguing in Publication Data.
A catalogue record for this book is available from the British Library.

ISBN 0 7524 2183 2

Typesetting and origination by Tempus Publishing Limited
Printed in Great Britain by Midway Colour Print, Wiltshire

Contents

To my father and mother

Acknowledgements

There are a number of people without whom this book would never have seen the light of day. Firstly, I'd like to thank everyone at Tempus Publishing for their immense patience; they have waited several years for me to assemble the content and then when I did eventually come up with the goods, their prompt, polite and professional approach has made the final months' work so much easier.

In addition, several other individuals have helped: Brian Doyle, who has forgotten more about St Johnstone than most others have ever known, has been his usual kind, organised and helpful self; Paul Fraser at St Johnstone provided a number of crucial photographs; Donald Farquhar can now get back the invitation the club issued to his relative Peter Jack for the Golden Jubilee in 1935, which is shown on page 91; and the studio at HR Gardens in Glasgow will no longer have to scan in long-lost photographs just to keep me happy.

Of course, I couldn't have done this without the help of a number of newspapers and their sports and photo departments. The *Perthshire Advertiser*, and in particular Gordon Bannerman, have provided the vast bulk of the photographs used, while the *Daily Record* and *Dundee Courier* have allowed me to use several other items.

Finally, my wife, Helen, and sons Peter and Andrew, have, as they have for many years, put up with me, supported, assisted and listened while I slowly assembled the necessary pictures, captions and other material. In return, I have made them all lifelong Saints fans.

Introduction

St Johnstone FC takes its name from the ancient name for Perth – Saint John's toun. Perth is, in many ways, a conservative, gentlemanly place and the surrounding county of Perthshire is an agricultural region of lovely contrasts, ranging from highland mountains to lowland farms and small agricultural towns. Industrial Scotland it certainly isn't, and the couth, kindly aspect of many of Perthshire's sons and daughters is very different from the somewhat harder aspects presented by cities such as Glasgow and Aberdeen. Despite this, major commercial concerns, such as John Dewar and Sons and General Accident have their origins in Perth and this is also one of the principal recruiting areas for the Black Watch. This amalgam of town and country, of steel and softness, makes it the most wonderful part of the world for everyone who has grown up there. Yet in some ways it is a strange place for a football club. Scottish football tends to pride itself on its craggy, industrial origins, whereas St Johnstone were formed from what most people (erroneously) believe to be that most English of pastimes, cricket. The St Johnstone Cricket Club, at a meeting in February 1885, were resolved to form a football club to keep their members active during the winter months. This activity has been almost continuous ever since (World Wars apart), yet the cricket club has been long since consigned to oblivion while the football club lives on.

From its origins in 1885, St Johnstone has been an interesting club; as the official history records it, 'Bristling with Possibilities'. For many years the Saints have prospered at the top level of Scottish football. Counterbalancing this, however, have been periods of slough and despondency, with occasions when the future of the club itself has been in question. Yet for the most part, times have been good. All that is missing is a major trophy. Despite several tilts at the final stage, St Johnstone have never won the Scottish Cup or League Cup, nor the Scottish top division Championship (variously First, Premier or SPL). Various divisional championships have been fairly regularly obtained, and two exciting trips into Europe have followed league campaigns in which St Johnstone has been the third best team in the country, but major silverware has not been forthcoming. At their best, the St Johnstone players have proved more than a match for any club, with both Celtic and Rangers experiencing a number of seasons during which a trip to Perth was fraught with danger. The local enemy, Dundee FC, provides another focal point for the Saints fans, with the despair of seeing the Dark Blues win the Scottish Championship at Muirton in 1962 more than offset (in Perth eyes), by a stunning 7-2 victory for Saints in the course of the 1996/97 First Division Championship-winning season.

Great players too, have enlivened many a Saturday afternoon or midweek evening. Current younger fans will rejoice in the evening of their lives by recalling 'The Legend', Roddy Grant, whereas a slightly older generation will (rightly!) aver that John Connolly was, and probably always shall be, the greatest, most skillful outfield player to don the club's royal-blue and white colours. For those of a slightly earlier vintage, the likes of Bill Taylor, Ernie Ewen or Paddy Buckley will be names to savour, yet no matter who is recalled, or whatever incidents or goals are discussed there is, as with all clubs, a common feeling of unity, of 'our' team and of tribal passion which is, I trust, unlikely ever to be dispersed by the commercial forces which increasingly assail our game.

In addition, there have been many players and officials who have passed, fleetingly or otherwise, through the portals of St Johnstone FC and have subsequently gone on to make a major impact on the game in the UK and internationally. The likes of Sir Alex Ferguson and Alistair McCoist, both of whom began their careers at Perth, are well known. And no other club has had two successive managers plucked from them by the SFA to manage the Scottish international side, as happened with Bobby Brown and Willie Ormond. Officials such as Robert Campbell, a player, director, president and chairman of the club have made their mark too. Campbell was president of the SFA at the time of the Wembley Wizards, while current chairman Geoff Brown has presided over a long and generally successful period in which his influence and stature have greatly benefited the club in its dealings with the wider football world.

This said, St Johnstone have been, for much of the history of the game in Scotland, an average to middling club – not quite big enough to be a fixture in the top league, yet with far too prosperous and interested a local constituency to fade into the permanent obscurity of the lower divisions. Perth is prosperous and recent history suggests that Saints are worthy of a place at the high table. The continually changing structure of the Scottish game may militate against this, but now, more than ever before, money is at the root of all the problems of football in our country and St Johnstone is a well-run and financially cautious company. At the time of writing, there are storm clouds on the horizon, yet football history and experience both teach that not much changes. We've seen it before, and will doubtless see it again. So long as the spirit that inspired the club's founders is still there, then St Johnstone will continue to be an important part of the Scottish game. So long as the likes of George Valentine, Robert Campbell and Geoff Brown give so freely of their time and abilities for the football club of Perth and Perthshire, and for its fans, at home or spread across the globe, then this, our football team, will survive – and occasionally thrive.

One
Historic Moments

The first photograph of St Johnstone in action, taken at the Recreation Grounds in 1885. Saints are in the dark shirts. Note the one-armed throw-in.

There was a Scotsman, an Englishman, an Irishman – and a Welshman! From left to right, Englishman Pocock, Scotsman McBain, Irishman Joe Toner, and Welshman Kirby. Joe Toner was the first Saints player to be capped, playing for Ireland in 1926 and 1927.

Wee Saints mascot, James Cattanach, in St Johnstone's change colours of maroon, presents a sprig of white heather to George Mason before the 1934 Scottish Cup semi-final *v.* Rangers.

The Lord Provost presents the Second Division trophy to Mr Lamond, chairman, in front of Bobby Brown and his players in May 1960.

The St Johnstone and West Ham United teams line up prior to the official opening of the Muirton Park floodlights. This game was played on 16 December 1964 and West Ham won 4-3. Saints are in the white tracksuits.

The Muirton dressing room after the side beat Dundee in the Scottish Cup in 1965. Neil Duffy, who scored the winner, is pictured at the back, second from the left.

The League Cup final, 1969. Celtic's Bertie Auld has just scored what proved to be the only goal of the game.

SHOCK—THEN JIM PEARSON STRIKES

HAMBURG...2   ST. JOHNSTONE...1

ONE of the worst decisions ever seen in Europe put St Johnston behind in this torrid tie in the Volkspark Stadium here tonight.

With Saints rattling the Germans with the attacking soccer they have become famous for, they were hit by a body blow in only the 10th minute.

The Perth side moved swiftly out of defence catching five German forwards in their offside trap.

CASUAL

The linesman clearly signalled for the infringement. But Zaczyk ran on and casually flicked the ball into the net with keeper Jim Donaldson making absolutely no effort to save.

To the astonishment and anger of St Johnstone the referee allowed the goal to stand, ruling that the ball had touched a Perth defender on the way through.

Saints protested vigorously but the referee refused to consult the linesman.

The goal was enough to dishearten the most experienced side in Europe. But these Saints babes, making their debut in Europe, fought back magnificently.

In fact, before that dreadful goal, Connolly came within inches of scoring with a tremendous 20 yard drive.

In the 17th minute Pearson and McPhee worked a quick one-two on the edge

FROM IAN BROADLEY HAMBURG, WEDNESDAY

of the box for the latter to send a drive inches wide.

Three minutes later, Donaldson made a brilliant save at the near post from left-back Kurbjuhn.

CLASH

In 29 minutes Hamburg's Swedish keeper Kargus was carried off with a dislocated elbow after an aerial clash with Jim Pearson.

He was replaced by Ozcan, and the angry Germans toughened up their play and the referee did nothing to control them.

There were further nasty scenes when Ozcan went down when challenged by Connolly and the Saints' forward was immediately surrounded by Hamburg defenders.

JUSTICE

But justice was done for this St Johnstone side just eight minutes after the restart.

John Lambie carried the ball down the right-wing past several players before crossing.

The ball struck a defender on the way catching Ozcan out of position and young Jim Pearson coolly sidefooted the ball into the net, to put his side level.

This was the reward Saints so richly deserved and they assumed command.

When it became obvious that St Johnstone were more than holding their

own, the German fans turned on them.

Indeed when John Connolly scratched the bar with a header, they applauded.

In the 67th minute, there was more trouble when Connolly was floored and needed treatment.

In 75 minutes St Johnstone were denied a penalty when Pearson was clearly brought down by Ripp when he seemed certain to score

But after all their pressure Saints fell behind once again in 80 minutes.

Hamburg—Kargus; Sandmann, Kurbjuhn, Kaltz, Ripp; Zaczyk, Nogly, Hallfritz; Bjornmose, Sealar, Winkler.

Subs.: Ozcan, Memering, Lubeque.

St. Johnstone—Donaldson; Lambie, Gordon, Rennie, Coburn; Rooney, McPhee; Aird, Pearson, Connolly, Hall.

Subs.: Aitken, Muir, Whitelaw, Argue, Robertson.

Referee—A. Ribeiro, Portugal.

The first ever competitive European match, as reported by the *Daily Record*.

Often seen, never forgotten. Saints' first goals at home in European competition, from Hall (top), Pearson (middle), and Whitelaw (bottom), from the 1971/72 season.

A minor crowd invasion at Alloa, as Saints clinch promotion from the First Division in 1983. Andy Brannigan (in the foreground, left) and Ray Blair seem fairly animated, while Jim Morton, standing behind them, looks dejected for some reason!

Manager Alex Rennie salutes the support at Muirton after the result of the final game of the 1983 season, against Dunfermline, clinches the title.

Alex Rennie, flanked by Rab Kilgour (left) and John Pelosi (right) in the dressing room, with the customary bottle of champagne, shows his elation at winning promotion.

Walking down the Dunkeld Road to see the Muirton Aces. The old ground, looking quite sprightly, on the day of the last-ever match to be staged there, against Ayr United on the 29 April 1989.

LAST MATCH
AT
MUIRTON PARK
ST. JOHNSTONE
v.
AYR UNITED
29th APRIL, 1989 – PERTH

29th APRIL, 1989
SCOTTISH B&Q LEAGUE
DIVISION ONE
ST. JOHNSTONE v. AYR UNITED
MUIRTON PARK, PERTH

St. Johnstone F.C., Muirton Park, Perth PH1 5AP

A special production by the Post Office – a 'last-day cover' (envelope and stamp) for Muirton Park's last-ever match.

A rare sight in Muirton's last few years – the fans queue up for the last-ever game, against Ayr. Note the floodlights have already been removed for relocation to the new ground.

Spot the ball – Saints and Ayr United players look everywhere but the right place! Action from the last-ever game at Muirton Park against Ayr United.

The official opening of McDiarmid Park. Manchester United are the visitors and here club captains Bryan Robson and Don McVicar pose for pictures with the mascots and pennants.

Counting down the minutes to the final whistle in the championship-winning game against Ayr United on 5 May 1990. Manager Alex Totten and his assistant, Bert Paton, feel the strain in the dugout. Sammy Johnston and Steve Maskrey, both in the foreground, look a bit more confident. Saints won 2-0 to gain promotion to the Premier Division.

The St Johnstone players celebrate on the pitch at Somerset Park, Ayr, after clinching the First Division Championship in 1990. From left to right: Gary McGinnis, Mark Treanor, Ian Heddle, Jimmy Peacock (physiotherapist), Roddy Grant, Allan Moore and Paul Cherry.

Mark Treanor steers home the penalty in the 5-0 rout of Aberdeen on 29 September 1990.

Saints stalwart and fans favourite, Paul Cherry, hoisted on Jim Weir's shoulders after his last game for the club, a scoreless draw at Dens on 4 May 1996.

The Saints players, inspired by Attila Sekerlioglu (far right of picture) and his famous post-match celebrations, raise the roof after beating East Fife at McDiarmid in 1997 to regain their Premier Division status.

The scene in the dressing room after the game, with manager Paul Sturrock getting the traditional soaking in champagne.

The League Cup final, 1998. Nick Dasovic turns away, pursued by George O'Boyle, after the former had scored Saints' goal in the 2-1 defeat by Rangers.

The Saints players, in the McDiarmid Park dressing room, celebrate qualification for Europe in 1999. They have just beaten age-old rivals Dundee 1-0.

Back into Europe after a thirty-year absence and the Jeanfield Supporters' Club get in the party mood at Vaasa in Finland.

The small coterie of journalists file their reports from the back of the trim wee stand in Vaasa.

A Saints fan gets some face paint in the club colours in preparation for the Monaco game.

Monaco meets the Saints, with the aid of some liquid refreshment.

Two

Grounds

*This chapter shows some of the grounds in Scotland where Saints have played over the years.
In particular, there is an emphasis on grounds which no longer exist,
or have changed considerably in recent years.*

St Johnstone's first home: the Recreation Grounds on the Edinburgh Road. The picture shows action from the first ever First Division game there, on 23 August 1924, against Falkirk. The Saints players are (in the white shorts), from left to right: Ribchester, Fleming and Glancy.

A towering stand, a handful of supporters and opponents with Ferranti on their jerseys – it's got to be Meadowbank Thistle at the Commonwealth Stadium, with Gordon Scott causing consternation amidst the home defence in a match during the 1984/85 season.

The same game at the former Commonwealth Stadium, this time with an unidentifiable Saints player, almost on the line, forcing the ball home – despite a desperate attempt to keep it out.

From the relative modernity of Meadowbank to one of the real former landmarks of British football – the Pavilion at Airdrie's Broomfield Stadium. In this 1980s action photograph, Andy Brannigan challenges for the ball. Note the unusual floodlight on the stand roof.

Broomfield again, with the inestimable Brogie being shut out by two Diamonds defenders.

Saints (in the hoops) take on East Stirling at Firs Park in the 1950s. Firs Park is notable for being the site of the smallest-ever crowd to watch St Johnstone – just 110 on 5 March 1986.

Dramatic poses from everyone, but the ball is nowhere to be seen as Billy Gavine stoops to get in a header at Clyde's former ground, Shawfield Park. The lights for the greyhound racing are more impressive than the crowd.

Tom McNeil weaves his magic in front of a sparse crowd in the stand at Boghead. The state of the weather can be gauged by the fact that the standing supporters are all huddled against the stand wall.

Boghead again, and Dumbarton's ground shows the traditional empty terrace, trees, decaying terraces and crush barriers that used to (and sometimes still do) characterise many stadia in the lower divisions in Scotland.

John Brogan adopts a classic pose at his home-town stadium. Douglas Park, Hamilton Accies' former ground, is now, like Muirton, the site of a supermarket.

At Hamilton again, this time a season or two later and a winter game on a less-than-perfect surface. Stuart Beedie fires the ball in, while the spectators at the other end huddle together for warmth.

A ground which still exists, but no longer has any standing areas. Dundee United's Tannadice Park is packed in the corners to see Micky Lyons tangle for the ball with current Saints assistant manager, Billy Kirkwood. Saints lost 7-0 in this match on 12 November 1983. Drew Rutherford and Alex Caldwell are looking on.

Tannadice again, with the old-fashioned half-time scoreboard on the flood-light pylon forming the backdrop as Jim Morton and David Narey go for the ball.

A scattering of fans at the 'away' end at East End Park, Dunfermline – now a modern stand – while in the foreground John Brogan turns away from his marker.

Jim Morton challenges the Pars 'keeper in front of the distinctive former East End Park advertising hoardings with their gap at the bottom.

Drew Rutherford watches as the ball is cleared by the Raith Rovers defence at Starks Park, Kirkcaldy. Raith's ground still retains its original stand, but the rest of the stadium has changed considerably since this picture was taken, with new stands all around. Note the unusual floodlight gantry.

One of the features of Starks Park is the railway line running along one side of the ground. In the foreground, John Brogan homes in on goal.

Another feature at Raith is the free view offered to the flats on Pratt Street, probably the most unfortunate address in senior football in the United Kingdom!

John Pelosi is thwarted by the Raith Rovers defence.

The first of four pictures from Falkirk FC's Brockville Stadium in the 1980s. They illustrate some of the typical archaic elements of older Scottish grounds. Here, you can see the ancient floodlights, empty terraces and Brogie shooting for goal.

Brogan rounds the goalkeeper, to a backdrop of dismayed home fans on the right and soon-to-be rejoicing Saints supporters on the left. Behind them there is the typical housing that surrounds Brockville.

Rutherford and Brannigan contest a corner at Falkirk. The faint remnants of an advertisement adorn the gable end of the house, the wall of which forms part of the boundary to the park.

No holding back from John Weir, with chimneys and advertisements in the background.

A steep terrace, angled at the top with the usual posse of Saintees sitting and standing to watch Tom McNeil fire in a shot against Hibernian at Easter Road. This League Cup match was played on 8 August 1981, Saints winning 2-1.

Looking down the famous Easter Road slope from the away terracing. This game was played during the Christmas period in 1990 (29 December to be exact), when Saints had returned to the Premier Division under Alex Totten. They won 1-0 on this occasion.

September 1984 and former Saint Kenny McDonald forces a great save from Gordon Drummond at Station Park, Forfar. In the background, fans sit on walls and the exit doors are the familiar corrugated iron, common at many Scottish grounds. Saints lost the match 4-0.

The same stadium and the same season, but this time it's March 1985. From left to right we see Sludden, McGurn, Lyons and Scott being beaten to the ball by the Forfar goalkeeper. On this occasion, the Saints won 1-0.

A famous Scottish sight – the hedge at Brechin. Four fans are apparently pausing on the way out to watch the ball sail over the bar as the home defence anxiously look on.

The same match in 1984, with Alex Caldwell indulging in some fairly entertaining contortions in an attempt to get to the ball.

The impressive tannoy horns at Kilbowie Park, Clydebank, with the small pavilion below and Ally McCoist about to pull the trigger.

John Brogan challenging alongside an unidentifiable Saints player at Kilbowie. Although now long gone as a venue for football, the Bankies' ground was the first ever all-seater stadium in the United Kingdom, albeit with bench seats in a wide variety of stands.

Some bigger crowds at Tynecastle, with Derek Addison whispering something to John Brogan while the Hearts defence get on with clearing the ball.

Saints' Raymond Blair takes on young Jambo, Gary Mackay. In the background is the Tynecastle 'away' end, with the tunnels through to the exits and turnstiles on the far right.

Andy Brannigan challenges at Tynecastle. At the far end is now the stand which houses the away supporters, while the old main stand is much the same as it is today.

Another big ground, but Celtic Park is sparsely filled in the upper tier of the main stand. The edge of the 'away' terracing, now replaced by stands, is just visible on the extreme right. John Brogan and Jim Morton are forging an attack.

The biggest expanse of empty terrace in Scotland: Hampden's slopes form the background to Andy Brannigan's attempt on goal – but there is not one fan in sight!

Hampden again, with Brogie challenging, watched by a small knot of loyal Saints, lost amidst the bowl of the stadium. The national stadium in these days was, it must be said, rather uninspiring as a venue, but it has now been substantially renovated and is fit for European finals once more.

Bayview, the former home of East Fife. Andy Brannigan is firing in a shot.

The same evening match, this time looking up the park, as Saints defend their lines.

The Scottish Cup can occasionally mean trips to slightly less substantial grounds. Here, Jim Morton holds off a Gala Fairydean player at the Borders club's trim little park. This game was played on 6 February 1982 and Saints won 2-1.

Umbrellas for the less hardy supporters as Stuart Beedie strokes the ball home at Gala.

Rugby Park, Kilmarnock was a huge barracks of a place, with an enormous, curved terrace for the away fans, although there weren't many on this occasion to watch John Brogan and his colleagues.

The same game, from the 1981/82 season, looking up the pitch towards a superb, traditional half-time scoreboard. Now it's all seated modernity at Killie, with stands all round.

Muirton Park, the club's home from 1924 until 1989. Here is an action shot from a snow-encrusted game during the 1952/53 season, when Saints had Johnny Pattillo as their first player-manager. The enclosure opposite the main stand wasn't built until the 1960s.

Sadly, perhaps inevitably, Muirton became a rather decrepit old stadium in its later days.

For the majority of Saints fans, 'home', from 1924 to 1989, meant Muirton Park. This picture shows the grandstand and enclosure below under construction, in the summer of 1924. Ladders rather than hydraulic cranes were the order of the day in the 1920s and cantilevers were not practicable then either.

Sixty-five years later and it's time for the construction of the Saints' new home in the spring of 1989. The steel superstructure for the main stand is in place, the pitch is laid out over Bruce McDiarmid's fields and cranes tower over the scene.

Three

Teams

The first St Johnstone team to win a trophy. Pictured in 1889, the Saints players show off the Reid Cup. At first glance this might seem to be a cricket club, but it is presumed that the team were posing in cricket whites, complete with pads, caps and bats, in recognition of the club's origins as St Johnstone Cricket Club.

It is the 1889/90 season and Saints have won the Perthshire FA Cup for the first time. From left to right, back row: Peter Smith (trainer), ex-Lord Provost McNab, John Robertson, David Tulloch, David Elliot, William Cattanach. Middle row: George Watson, Robert Winton, Thomas Rodger. Front row: George Smith, George Burnfield, Ben Waddell, David Burnfield, Andrew McFarlane.

The 1894/95 season, and a classic, posed nineteenth-century picture of the side which won the Perthshire FA and Reid Cups.

The same trophies were won again in 1896. Note that at this time, Saints were playing in white jerseys – the blue and white didn't come into use until the 1890s, and then it was blue and white hoops rather than the solid blue tops we know today. From left to right, back row: James Goodall, John Robertson, D. Tulloch, Dakers, A. Moncrieff, J. Gordon. Middle row: Colin Stewart, P. Hill, Alex King, Tom McFarlane, Peter Baxter, Alex Gow (trainer). Front row: William McFarlane, Ben Waddell, Andrew Moir, David Anderson. There are several notable figures here: John Robertson was the first Saints player to have an international trial, while Peter Baxter was a local Baillie and author of the first book on Perthshire football.

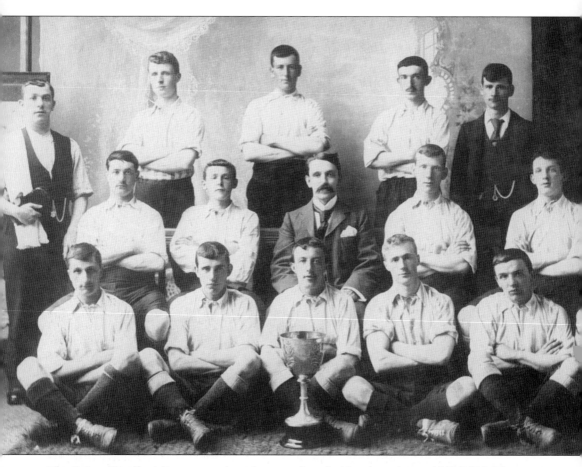

The Saints 'Strollers' (i.e. reserves), with an unidentified local trophy, in 1889/1900. The man in the suit at the far right in the back row is believed to be a youthful Robert Campbell, who is arguably the single most important figure in St Johnstone's history.

Outside the Recreation Grounds pavilion in 1911, with the Scottish Consolation Cup, the Dewar Shield and the Perthshire FA Cup. From left to right, back row: Jackson, Aitken, Ferguson. Middle row: Bennet, Sampson, Cameron, Jock McVean (trainer), Robert Campbell (in shirt and tie). Front row: Wilson, Hill, McKay, Stephen, Brown.

The Recreation Grounds were also used for the inter-county games that were popular at this time. Pictured here is the Perthshire select that took on Forfarshire in 1914.

St Johnstone FC in vertical stripes outside the pavilion at the Recreation Grounds, 1 May 1920. From left to right, back row: T. MacPherson, Allan Galloway (captain), Mr Peter Grant (manager), Pitt, Taylor, R. McCulloch, McInnes, Nicol. Front row: Robertson, T. McCulloch, Williams, Forbes, Sailor.

The St Johnstone team pictured around 1922 at the Recreation Grounds. Bunnets were mandatory for everyone apart from the players! Goalkeeper Alick Stewart's son also played for the club, as a winger in the 1930s.

Central FC, winners of the Norie-Miller Cup, in 1926. The team features Sandy McLaren, who was to go on to become (arguably) Saints' greatest-ever player, in goal.

A year later, and McLaren is the 'keeper for Tulloch Juveniles, who beat Methven in the County Cup final. From left to right, back row: Roberton, Fenton, McLaren, Farrel, Nicol. Front row: Malcolm, Montgomery, Mechie, Young, Band, Brown.

The 1923/24 Second Division championship-winning side, with the second Saints strip to feature a badge – in this case, the city's crest. Chairman Robert Campbell is sitting in the centre at the front.

Another photograph from the same season. From left to right, back row: Coyle, McRoberts, Stewart, Deuchar, Wilson. Front row: Ribchester, Walker, Fleming, Harvey, Hart, Donaldson.

Opposite: Following relegation in 1930, Saints finished sixth in the Second Division in 1930/31. This is the team that took part in the campaign. From left to right, back row: McBain, Bain, Ferguson, McLaren, Hogg, Steele. Front row: Cargill, Miller, Cameron, Deuchar, Nicholson.

Team photograph from the 1924/25 season, in which Bob Penman (seated centre front) became the first Saint to play 100 consecutive games for the club. From left to right, back row: McLean, McLure, Dempster, Thomson, White, Walker. Front row: Black, Dick, Penman, Hart, Swallow.

The team that regained top-flight status in 1932. From left to right, back row: Ferguson, Welsh, McLaren, Wilson, McBain, Ireland. Front row: Ritchie, Benzie, Benson, Nicol, Nicholson.

Sandy McLaren (back row, third from right) in the Scotland team that faced Wales on 22 October 1932. This was his last game playing for the international side.

One of the great Saints teams, 1934/35. From left to right, back row: Mason, Clark, Wylie, Taylor, Campbell, Moulds. Front row: Tennant, Davidson, Stewart, H. Ferguson, A. Ferguson. Inserts: Welsh, Dickie.

The team for the 1935/36 season, when Saints finished seventh in the First Division. From left to right, back row: J. Welsh, W. Clark, R. Wylie, D. Baxter, J. Littlejohn, J. Smeaton. Front row: J. Tennant, H. Adam, H. Lyle, H. Ferguson (captain), W. Nicholson.

After the war, Saints were 'relegated' to the B Division. The 1945/46 side featured a mixture of local juniors and more experienced men, including the great Sandy McLaren, who had returned from his wartime service in the Russian convoys. From left to right, back row: Hiddleston, Johnstone, McLaren, McGechie, Boyd. Front row: Blyth, Ireland, Burns, McIntosh, Crowe, Conway.

A few years later, Saints were still looking for promotion. From left to right, back row: McGowan, Woodcock, Christie, Hamilton, Innes, McColl. Front row: Goldie, McKinley, Andrews, Davies, Armitt.

By the 1956/57 season, Saints were making a reasonable challenge to be promoted to the First Division. There were, however, some who suggested that they didn't actually want to achieve promotion. This picture features some notable heroes from this time: Big 'Ming' (Menzies), a former Cowdenbeath defensive stalwart, Ernie Ewen, an accomplished right half, the all-time second top scorer, Ian Rodger, and Joe Carr. The line-up is, from left to right, back row: McFadyen, Montgomery, Ewen, McLaren, Baird, Menzies. Front row: Hodgson, Robertson, Steel, Whitelaw, Carr.

The end of the 1957/58 season and Saints line up in one of the flashiest strips of all time. From left to right, back row: McFadyen, Ewen (captain), Taylor, McKim, Baikie, Hawthorne. Front row: Gillespie, Hutcheson, McInnes, Rafferty, Carr.

The Second Division championship-winning squad, pictured with the Second XI Cup before the start of the 1961/62 season, which ended in promotion. This line-up features a man who would go on to become one of the most successful British managers ever. As well as Alex Ferguson, this squad contained the father of a man who would become the 'legend' of the 1990s – Roddy Grant. From left to right (players only), back row: Jim Ferguson, Bobby Grant, Jimmy Walker, Bill Taylor, Ian Gardiner, Jimmy Little, Ian Ower, Laurie Thomson. Middle row: Bobby Gray, Charlie McFadyen, Peter Campbell, Jimmy Lachlan, Bobby Wright, Bobby Gilfillan, Ron McKinven. Front row: Jim Menzies, Matt McVittie, John Soutar, Bobby Brown (manager), John Bell, Joe Carr, Joe Henderson, Alex Ferguson.

Saints team from the 1963/63 season. From left to right, back row: Cadenhead, Lachlan, Taylor, Jackson, Roe, McGarry. Front row: McIntyre, Flannigan, Harrower, Craig, Kemp.

Coming into the modern era, this Saints pre-season team defeated Ipswich 5-2 on the 6 August 1966. At this time, Ipswich were a mid-table team in the English Second Division. From left to right, back row: Littlejohn, McCarry, Michie, Ryden, Donaldson, McPhee, Coburn. Front row: Clark, Duffy, Rooney, Kilgannon, Kemp.

Another pre-season friendly against another English Second Division mid-table side, this time Preston North End. The Lancashire side won the match, played on 1 August 1969, 2-1. This photograph was handed out with the programme for the game. From left to right, back row: Willie Ormond (manager), Willie Coburn, Alex Gordon, Alex Tennie, Derek Robertson, Benny Rooney, Jimmy Donaldson, John Muir, Gordon Whitelaw, Fred Aitken, Frank Christie (trainer). Front row: Kenny Aird, Henry Hall, Buck McCarry, John Connolly, Ian McPhee.

The 1975 squad, who were to go on to establish a record low number of points for the Premier Division (11). From left to right, back row: Gordon McGregor, Lindsay Hamilton, John McIndoe, Andy Kinnell, Derek Robertson, Phil Roberts, Duncan McLeod, Middle row: John Lambie (coach), Sandy Smith, John Hotson, Gordon Murdoch, Tom McGurk, Stewart McBean, Vic Robertson, Atholl Henderson, Jim Peacock (physiotherapist). Front row: Bobby Thomson, Gordon Smith, Jim O'Rourke, Billy Ritchie, John Muir, Gordon Cramond, Duncan Lambie, -?-.

In 1980, another young Glaswegian was in the initial stages of his career with his first club. Unlike Alex Ferguson, Ally McCoist was a great player, whose early promise wasn't fulfilled until he moved from Sunderland (who bought him from Saints in 1981) to Rangers. McCoist is widely regarded as one of the all-time Ibrox greats. From left to right, back row: Frank Christie (coach), John Weir, George Fleming, John Mackay, Alex Caldwell, George Tulloch, Jim Docherty, Tom McNeil, Charlie Bates (physiotherapist). Front row: Rab Kilgour, Ally McCoist, John Pelosi, Alex Rennie (manager), Drew Rutherford, Jim Morton, John Brogan.

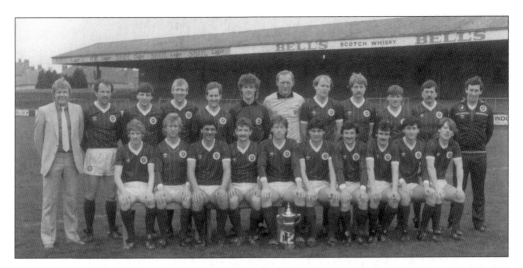

Alex Rennie's First Division Champions squad pictured in August 1983.

It took another seven years, following one of the worst ever periods in the club's history, before Saints regained their Premier Division status. In the meantime, the club nearly went out of business, only being saved by local businessman Geoff Brown. His first manager, Alex Totten, put together a good team, shown here prior to a Scottish Cup tie with Aberdeen in January 1988, when Saints were still in the Second Division (then the lowest level of the League). From left to right, back row: Sammy Johnston, Kenny Thomson, John Balavage, Alan McKillop, Tommy Coyle, Ian Heddle. Front row: Gary Thompson, Willie Watters, Don McVicar, Steve Maskrey, Dougie Barron.

An 'all-star' Saints XI took on a touring English side at McDiarmid Park in 1991. Some well-kent names took to the field, albeit a few pounds heavier than in the pomp of their playing days. From left to right, back row: Drew Rutherford, John Connolly, Fred Aitken, George Miller, Alec Gordon, Jim Donaldson, Andy Brannigan, Jim Pearson, Willie Coburn, John Blackley. Front row: Henry Hall, Gordon Whitelaw, Alex MacDonald, Jackie Coburn, Alex Totten. It would be interesting to speculate how this side might have got on if they had played together when at the peak of their powers. Certainly, the likes of Connolly, MacDonald, Hall, Pearson, and Blackley (and most of the rest) would walk straight into an SPL side nowadays, and probably into the national team too!

The Saints squad celebrate on their home pitch with the First Division trophy after the final game in the 1996/97 season.

Four
Now and Then

The boardroom in Muirton Park in the 1970s, featuring a rather well-used table and a selection of trophies and mementos. The large trophy is the Dewar Shield, first competed for in the late nineteenth century. Nowadays, this silverware is all carefully secured in a glass-fronted cabinet in the slightly more salubrious boardroom at McDiarmid Park.

The directors in 1952, from left to right: R.A. Sawers, A. Lamond, J. Dick, I.S. Campbell.

The directors, 1986/87. From left to right, back row: A. Campbell, A. Baillie, D. Sidey, H. Ritchie. Front row: G. Brown, A. Lamond.

The 1934 Scottish Cup semi-final against Rangers at Hampden.

The 1989 Scottish Cup semi-final against Rangers at Celtic Park. Sammy Johnston, flanked by Terry Butcher and Richard Gough, is pictured with Grant Jenkins in the background.

The St Johnstone FC supporters' club committee, 1952. From left to right: D. Imrie, W.D. Scrimgeour, W. Farrell.

The Supporters' Club, late 1960s. Henry Hall is seen receiving his Player of the Year trophy presented by Messrs S. McKinna (far right) and R. Fulton (centre). Robin Fulton's brother, Graham, was for many years the sports reporter for the *Perthshire Advertiser* (the local Perth paper), a job which, as far as he was concerned, was genuinely a case of a fan with a typewriter!

Training on 3 August 1933 – Davidson and Campbell take a break at Muirton.

Training 1950s style – 'Alright lads, this is the ball'. Jock Smeaton (far right) passes on advice to (from left to right) Craig, Buckley, Peat and Goldie.

Training in front of the Muirton Stand, October 1961.

Training during the infamous Kinnoull Hill pre-season: trainer Frank Christie (background left) puts Henry Hall and his colleagues through the mill in the late 1960s.

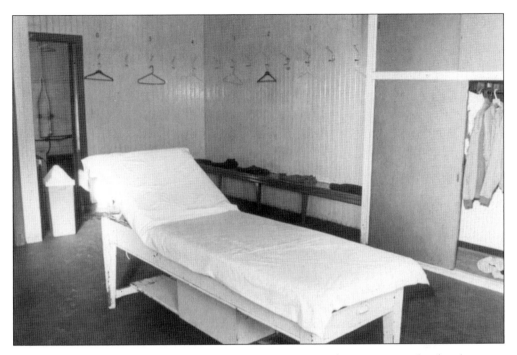

Physiotherapy – the old treatment table at Muirton seems to be just waiting for the electrodes to be attached.

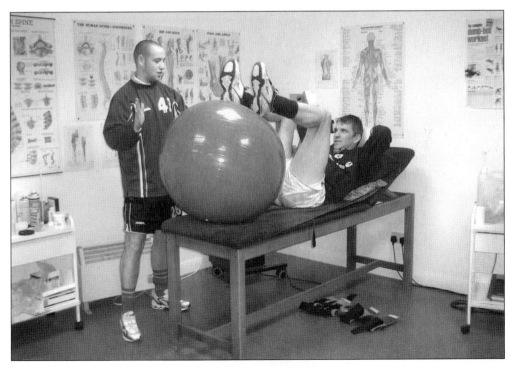

Physiotherapy – the ultra-modern treatment room under the West Stand at McDiarmid Park. No doubt in twenty years' time this will be considered as old-fashioned as the picture above is today.

Relaxing – the Saints players at Crieff Hydro in March 1968.

Relaxing – Programme cover showing Paul Sturrock's Saints prior to heading out for their Christmas party in 1993.

Relaxing – golf in the 1930s.

Relaxing – the Centenary Suite under the McDiarmid Park main stand in 1999, with Roddy Grant and John McQuillan entertaining former director Gus Stewart and his party.

Raising the flag – the occasion is the first home game of the 1924/25 season after Saints had won the Second Division championship the previous season.

Raising the flag – it is nearly forty years later, but the crowd in 1963 doesn't look too different as another Second Division flag is about to be run up the flagpole.

Fashion statements – the crowd for a match against Raith Rovers in 1917.

Fashion statements – the crowd for a match against Raith Rovers in 1979.

What the well-dressed players were wearing in the 1920s.

What the well-dressed players were wearing in the 1980s.

The OFFICIAL FOOTBALL PROGRAMME

For NORTHERN LEAGUE MATCHES - -

Played at the • •

ST. JOHNSTONE RECREATION GROUNDS,

EDINBURGH ROAD, PERTH.

DUNFERMLINE ATHLETIC

versus

ST. JOHNSTONE

SATURDAY, 19th Mar., 1904.   Kick=off at 3.45.

No. 10.   *Compiled by Smart & M'Kinlay, Printers and Publishers, Charterhouse Lane, Perth.*

The programme in 1904. This is a facsimile of a very old programme indeed, as not many were produced at this time and their survival is very much a matter of chance.

A special one-off programme for a ex-pros game in 1934, featuring, amongst others, Rangers and Scotland star Alan Morton, Saints' then manager Tommy Muirhead (also a former Ranger and Scotland international), and former Saints manager Davie Taylor.

The Football Match of the Year.

DUNDEE *v.* PERTH

EX-PROFESSIONALS

AT

MUIRTON PARK, PERTH,

ON

WEDNESDAY, 25th April, 1934.

The programme, as remembered by a generation from the 1960s.

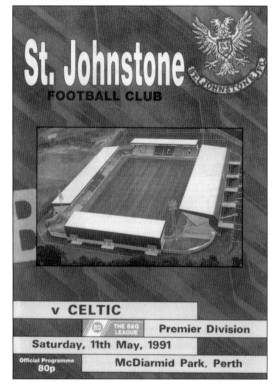

The programme for the last game of the 1990/91 season.

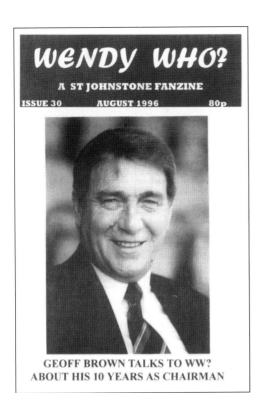

WENDY WHO?

A ST JOHNSTONE FANZINE

ISSUE 30   AUGUST 1996   80p

GEOFF BROWN TALKS TO WW?
ABOUT HIS 10 YEARS AS CHAIRMAN

The 1980s saw the emergence of fanzines. The first, and arguably the best, Saints fanzine was the wonderfully named *Wendy Who?*

100% unofficial

blue heaven

a st.johnstone fanzine

SERGEI

EXCLUSIVE interview

issue 1   february 2000   £1

Several other fanzines were produced, including *Old McDiarmid had a Farm*, *True Faith*, *The J Files* and the most recent, *Blue Heaven*.

Techniques for keeping the surface playable have varied over the years. Here, in the 1960s, a makeshift snowplough carves a path at the Ice Rink end of Muirton.

By the 1990s, an 'overblanket', or more accurately a set of heavy duty covers, helped (up to a point) to play games in spite of the Scottish winter. Nick Dasovic, the club's most capped player (26 for Canada), is seen with the covers after they have been rolled off the pitch.

Match mascots, as page 10 shows, have been with us for many decades. Here, despite the snow, is one delighted wee lad photographed in the 1980s with player-manager Ian Gibson.

It is not uncommon for more than one mascot to share the honour. In this photograph, two brothers are entertained by Tony Cole prior to the Dundee United game on 21 August 1993.

Advertising – famous local shop Joe Anderson's is featured in the *Topical Times Sporting Annual* of 1934/35. (For the benefit of younger readers, 20s (shillings) was equivalent to £1, and you could get an entire set of strips for 22s.)

Advertising – a match-programme promotion for the now defunct Saints shop in North Methven Street, formerly known as the St Johnstone Aid Club. Prices had gone up a bit, with the cheapest footballs now costing about six times more than their 1930s equivalents.

Five
Famous Saints

George Valentine, a cutler from Perth and one of the driving forces behind St Johnstone. He played an especially important role in the club getting access to Craigie Haugh, where the Recreation Grounds were sited. Seen here in a family picture, taken outside their house in High Craigie, George Valentine is second from the right in the middle row, behind the lady in the white blouse.

John Robertson, arguably the club's first great player. A full-back/defender, he was twice invited for trials for Scotland, even though Saints were still a non-League club at the time.

A twentieth-century photograph of Peter Baxter, who played in some of the early Saints teams of the 1880s and 1890s and who wrote *Football in Perthshire* – from which comes much of our knowledge of the club's early days.

TOM CAIRNS

Tommy Cairns, who was the first major signing by Rangers of a St Johnstone player. He only played from August 1913 until the middle of November, but went on to become one of Rangers' most successful players. For some reason, Saints have a tradition of providing Rangers with some excellent players. As well as Cairns, there have been the likes of Jimmy Fleming (see below), Alex McDonald and Alastair McCoist.

Jimmy Fleming (above and right), the next big signing by Rangers. He still holds the record for the Ibrox club of most goals in any one game, with 9 against Blairgowrie in a 14-2 win in the Scottish Cup on 20 January 1934.

A.S. Reid, the Airdrie player whose signing by St Johnstone after the transfer deadline led to the deduction of 2 points and Saints' failure to gain promotion in 1923.

Jimmy Benson, Saints' top scorer in any one season. His 38 goals in 1931/32 helped the club regain their First Division status, lost in 1930.

A group of Saints players at the Recreation Grounds in 1924. Centre, in the dark jersey, is the manager, Davie Taylor, who had a very successful playing career and is one of the very small number of professionals who have played for both Celtic and Rangers.

For many, Sandy McLaren is the most important St Johnstone player of all time. He was the club's first Scottish international cap and the third youngest cap of all time (and the youngest goalkeeper ever). Sandy was born in Tibbermore, just a few miles outside Perth on Christmas Day in 1910 and signed professional forms for St Johnstone 17 years later (to the very day). Just over a year later, he was making his Scotland debut aged 18 years and 152 days. A move to Leicester was followed by wartime service in the navy, including time spent on the Artic convoys. After the war, he played a handful of games for St Johnstone in the 1940s. He died in 1960.

Cigarette card featuring Harry Ferguson. Harry, who came from the Hillfoots district of Clackmannanshire, was probably the most loyal Saints player of all time. His twelve seasons at Perth spanned from 1925 to 1937, and in that time he played 285 times, scoring 70 goals. He is St Johnstone's joint record scorer (along with Steve Maskrey) in the Scottish Cup, having scored 7 goals.

Bob Penman, the first Saints player to record 100 consecutive appearances in competitive games for the club, beginning on the first day of the 1924/25 season against Rangers and reaching the century on 11 December 1926.

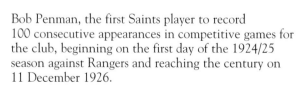

Peter Jack, groundsman and occasional trainer to St Johnstone from the 1930s to 1960. He is pictured here (centre) in 1954 with new signings Montgomery and McIntyre.

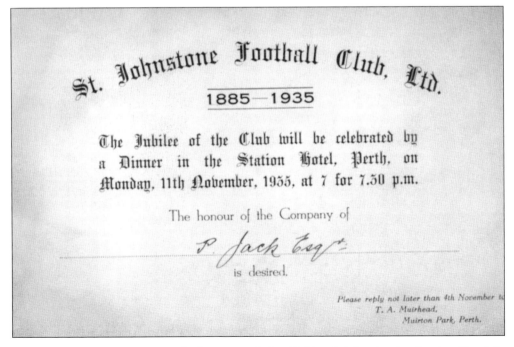

St. Johnstone Football Club, Ltd.

1885—1935

The Jubilee of the Club will be celebrated by a Dinner in the Station Hotel, Perth, on Monday, 11th November, 1935, at 7 for 7.30 p.m.

The honour of the Company of

P. Jack Esq.

is desired.

Please reply not later than 4th November to
T. A. Muirhead,
Muirton Park, Perth.

The club's invitation to Peter Jack to attend the Golden Jubilee in the Station Hotel in November 1935.

Left and *right*: Robert Campbell – player, president, director, chairman and probably the single most important person in the club's history. He was also president of the SFA at the time of the Wembley Wizards. The first of these photographs was taken before the First World War, the second in the early 1930s.

LATE MR ROBERT CAMPBELL

An Appreciation

SIR JAMES LEISHMAN writes:–

A very large number of people, in almost every section of society, will note with deep regret the passing of Mr Robert Campbell, of Perth.

Few men in the circle of legal and banking and sporting activities have earned and deserved such real appreciation and esteem for competent and sustained services. Many of these services were freely rendered from an abiding sense of duty and desire to give to the public the best that was in him of knowledge and wisdom.

Mr Campbell had an almost consuming desire to help all with whom he came in contact, and more especially the young men of the day. In nearly all kinds of sport he took a great interest, and probably most of all in Association football. As a player, committee man, and legislator, Mr Campbell played an important part. His great desire was to see the game developed on sound lines, and to see it well played as a clean, honest sport and he was intensely anxious to ward off any influences which he thought might do harm to the game, which he wished to see played in the true spirit of sport, and for exercise, recreation, and the cultivation of the spirit of comradeship and fair play.

Some years ago, Mr Campbell, along with Mr Furst and Mr Graham, were appointed by the Scottish Football Association to appear before the Royal Commission on Lotteries and Betting. I well remember the powerful effect produced by this able deputation. These gentlemen created a deep impression on the members of the Commission, and at the time I noted the sense of relief and immense satisfaction that was felt by the Commission that the great game of football had produced in Scotland such public-spirited and able guardians of the great sport of the people.

An able, genial, kindly Scot has gone from us – a friendly, social man, a man of public spirit, a fine citizen, and a "good sport."

The obituary for Robert Campbell that appeared in *The Times*. No other St Johnstone player or official has featured in this way.

Tommy Muirhead and Bobby Davidson, with Smith and Fulton standing at the back of the photograph. Muirhead was Saints' first great manager, taking his 1930s team to the top reaches of the First Division. Davidson was a typical inside forward: small, tough and with a great shot. He was transferred to Arsenal in 1935.

Paddy Buckley was a dynamite centre forward. Diminutive, hard and very fast, he scored 105 goals for Saints during the 1950s before a move to Aberdeen and international recognition for Scotland. He is shown here (centre) scoring a typical goal in a home game at Muirton.

Ian Rodger was signed in 1953 from Aberdeen to score goals. He did this very effectively, his 116 goals putting him second behind John Brogan in the club's goal-scoring chart.

Big Billy Taylor was a superb and brave goalkeeper. Taylor, plus full-backs Lachlan and McFadyen, were the names most fans wanted to hear first when the team was announced over the PA at Muirton in the early 1960s.

94

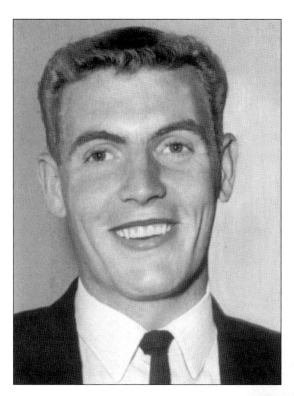

Jim Townsend was an inside forward whose talents led to him being transferred to Middlesbrough for a record fee of £20,000 in 1963. He returned to Perth in 1966 for £9,000 and was then sold on to Hearts in 1967 for £20,000.

One of many Saints who have gone on to great success at Rangers, Alex MacDonald was described by his peers at Perth as one of the most skilful players they had ever seen.

Bobby Brown, the second great St Johnstone manager, who guided the club back to the First Division after a lengthy post-war period in the doldrums. He also oversaw several great cup runs to the semi-final stage and became Scotland manager in 1966. This picture, taken in February 1967, shows him surrounded by his players at the piano.

Willie Ormond, Saints' greatest manager in many people's eyes, took the team to their first domestic final (the League Cup in 1969) and also into Europe for the first time in 1971. He succeeded Bobby Brown as Scotland manager in 1973.

The great Ormond side featured the incomparable talents of Connolly, Hall, Aird and Aitken – the finest forward combination in the club's history – snapped here in March 1969 after training.

John Connolly: for those who saw him play, the greatest, most skilful outfield player ever to don the club's colours.

Jim Pearson, another Ormond success, played at centre forward with Hall, Connolly et al and eventually joined Connolly at Everton.

Jimmy Donaldson, seen here saving a penalty at the Nep Stadium against Vasas Budapest in the UEFA Cup in 1971. Jimmy's spectacularly entertaining approach to the custodian's art endeared him to a generation of fans.

Henry Hall might not hold the all-time record number of goals for Saints, but there is no doubt he is the club's greatest ever goalscorer. All of his 114 goals were scored at the very highest levels, including the first home goal in Europe.

Mary Gibson, pictured in the Muirton kitchens with husband James in 1981. She first worked for the club in 1947 and, as the official tea lady, looked after generations of Saints' players.

Alistair McCoist was yet another Saint who went on to Ibrox and much greater things. In McCoist's case this move was made via Sunderland, who had been attracted by his precocious talents and parted for a then record fee to Saints of £355,000. He is shown here rounding a Hibs defender to score in a League Cup game on 8 August 1981.

The man who taught McCoist everything he knew, the one and only John Brogan. For many of the present-day generation of Saints fan, he is the best goalscorer they have seen. His 140 goals is the club record and unlikely to be overhauled for some time.

Manager Alex Rennie, pictured in May 1983 with his captain, Alex Caldwell, holding the First Division trophy. Rennie was a stylish left half in Willie Ormond's day, who as manager guided the club back to the top flight, albeit only for one season.

Drew Rutherford, the formidable 1980s centre-back who holds the all-time record for number of appearances with 345 (including 5 as substitute). He is seen here with a police escort to help get through the Saints fans after clinching promotion at Alloa in 1983.

Sammy Johnston was a highly skilful midfielder who helped Alex Totten's Saints achieve much of their success. This picture was taken during his days in the 1985 youth team.

Stevie Maskrey, the speedy winger whose displays brightened up many an afternoon for Saints fans. His goal against Raith Rovers on 13 August 1988 is probably one of the best ever scored by a St Johnstone player. This well-known photograph shows him scoring the goal against Ayr United that guaranteed Saints promotion in 1990.

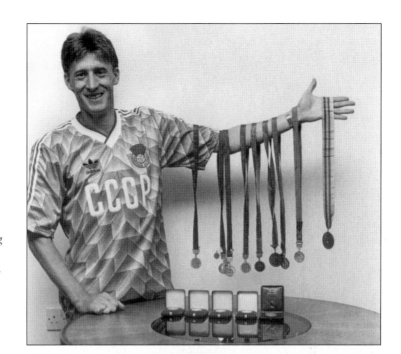

Sergei Baltacha, the Ukranian sweeper, came to Perth at the tail-end of a glittering career, with over 50 caps for the USSR and a host of medals, including a European Cup Winners Cup medal from his days with Dynamo Kiev.

Paul Wright, a superb goalscorer whose hammer-like shot and quick feet enabled him to score 51 goals for the club between 1991 and 1994. He is pictured here disputing the ownership of his jersey with Motherwell's Chris McCart.

Harry Curran, a popular and free-scoring midfielder, was the scorer of the first ever St Johnstone goal at McDiarmid Park, on 19 August 1989.

The legendary Roddy Grant, a centre forward of immense skill and slowness, but one of the most popular ever cult figures at St Johnstone. Roddy made 291 appearances (222+69 as a substitute) and scored 79 goals.

Two pictures of Roddy in the promotion-winning season of 1996/97 – in the act of shooting for goal from the penalty mark, and then turning to receive the acclaim of the massed crowds in the West Stand at McDiarmid.

Danny Griffin, seen here at the start of his career with one of his Northern Ireland youth caps. A superb defender, he became St Johnstone's youngest captain when he was skipper for the first team at St Mirren on 26 August 1995 at the age of 18 years and 16 days. Even more amazingly, he had played only 6 (yes, 6) first-team games!

Callum Davidson, who unusually for a footballer was offered a university place to study engineering. He could also have been a professional golfer, but opted for football and left Saints for Blackburn for a record fee of £1.75 million in February 1998. He was subsequently capped for Scotland and now plays for Leicester City.

Saints are fortunate in having had two great 'tea ladies'. The indefatigable Aggie Moffat has taken on the torch from Mary Gibson and is held in the same esteem and affection by all the staff and players, as demonstrated in this picture to mark her twenty years of service to the club.

Geoff Brown – the man who saved St Johnstone. In 1986 he assumed control of the then financially stricken club, which was in the football doldrums, and he has remained at the helm ever since, overseeing some of the best years in the club's history. Here, Geoff (on the left) is pictured alongside arguably his most successful manager, Paul Sturrock.

Jim Weir has been a rock at the heart of the Saints defence since 1994, in the great tradition of Drew Rutherford, Alex Gordon, Frank Moulds et al. Jim is one of those (relatively few) footballers who through time have developed a real allegiance to his club. He is seen here in the sweet aftermath of winning the First Division championship in 1997.

Alan Main, who holds the record of eight consecutive shutouts in League matches (a Saints record), achieved during the promotion season of 1996/97, seen here in training on the North Inch. In the opinion of many, not just St Johnstone supporters, it is a scandal that he has never been capped for his country. After 273 games for the club, Alan was transferred to Livingston in January 2002.

Six

The Glorious Game

The third home game of the 1924/25 season and Hibs are in the process of scoring at the Recreation Grounds (Saints are in the hoops).

The Boy Benson, Saints' record League goalscorer in one season (38 in 1931/32), seen second from the right in a cup replay at Perth on 20 January 1932; Saints beat Ayr United 2-0. The other Saints players are Nicol (left foreground) and Benzie. In the next round, Saints were paired with Celtic and went down 4-2 in a game at Perth which was watched by nearly 20,000 spectators.

A skirmish in front of goal leads to Saints' third goal in a 5-2 win over Alloa at Muirton on 24 January 1948.

Action from the post-war B Division game against Dunfermline on 5 February 1949, as the ball swirls past the visitors' goal from a corner. The Pars went on to win 2-1.

The first game of the next season and Saints beat Kilmarnock 3-2 in the League Cup game at Muirton on 13 August. The Killie 'keeper is shown clutching the ball as Paddy Buckley moves in.

In front of a 7,000 crowd, McKinlay scores the first goal of a hat-trick in a 5-2 demolition of Ayr, 7 January 1950.

Paddy Buckley, one of the all-time great Saints goalscorers, is defied by Kilmarnock 'keeper Niven. The action took place at Muirton on 10 March 1951.

Action in a 6-0 drubbing from Queen of the South at Muirton, 7 April 1951. This shot shows one of Saints' few attacks.

A goal direct from a corner, this time for Saints in a match on the 8 December 1951. This was one of three from Brydon in a 6-0 rout of Cowdenbeath.

Action from the same 6-0 win over Cowdenbeath. Here, Buckley scores Saints' third goal despite the despairing dive of the visitors' goalie.

Saints wing-half, McCall, gets in behind Albion Rovers' deputy 'keeper. Although he missed the ball, it still hit the post and went into the net! The game took place in February 1952.

1 March 1952 and Saints
'keeper, Stephen, in his only
game for the first team, is
pushed over by Alloa centre
Hamilton. The ball entered
the net directly from the
corner kick.

To prove that raised arms are
nothing new, Saints inside
forward Forsyth is shown
here on the receiving end
from a Hamilton Accies
defender in a match at
Muirton on 22 March 1952.

A pre-season trial match at Muirton in the summer of 1952. Davies (right) and Andrew are shown in front of a sparse crowd of dedicated fans.

A goal-line clearance by a Morton defender in the game on 4 October 1952. Saints won 3-1.

Sometimes it's easier to score ... Here, trialist inside right Baird balloons over the bar in a game against Arbroath on 27 February 1954. This miss did not matter, however, as Saints still won 3-0.

A trialist right-winger, Doig, scores against Dundee United on 18 September 1954.

Saints going down 1-0 to Alloa on 16 October 1954. In the last minute of the game, Ian Rodger sends a screamer inches over the bar.

A trialist goalkeeper (Budd) shows his prowess in a 1-0 home defeat against Albion Rovers on 30 October 1954.

Ian Rodger scores against
Ayr, 13 November 1954.
Saints won the match 2-1.

Another of Ian Rodger's
many goals for Saints.
Here, the Arbroath
defence look on as the
ball enters the net in
a Scottish Cup tie on
28 September 1955.

26 Feb 1955 and a Baird shot is well saved by the Cowdenbeath goalkeeper. Saints lost 4-0.

Taylor, Lachlan, McFadyen – the three names which were always first on the team sheet in the early 1960s. Here, Charlie McFadyen helps out 'keeper Taylor by heading this Queen of the South effort off the line.

Something every Saints fan enjoys – a winning goal over Dundee. Neil Duffy's lob sails over the 'keeper and into the net during a 1965 Scottish Cup match.

A superb drive from Jim Townsend gives Saints a half-time lead against Rangers, despite Martin's athletic dive. This match at Muirton on 19 November 1966 ended in a 1-1 draw.

2 January 1969. Saints 3, Aberdeen 1 – here Fred Aitken in full flight nearly gets another goal.

Fearless Fred Aitken (seen on the extreme right) scores his third goal against Arbroath on 25 January 1969.

Muirton Park, full of only Saints fans. It's 20 October 1971, the second round of the UEFA Cup and Jim Pearson gets between two Vasas Budapest defenders to direct a header towards goal. The author is somewhere above the ground-level Bell's advertising hoarding.

A perfect Jim Morton penalty, taken against Queen of the South on 27 February 1982.

2 October 1982,
and Andy Branni-
gan shows typical
determination
during a 4-0 win
over Falkirk.

Don McVicar, watched from the sidelines by substitute Andy Brannigan, prepares to clear his lines at Ibrox during the 1983/84 season.

Alan Lyons has put the ball in the net, to the dismay of Rangers 'keeper McCloy, but the goal was disallowed. Saints lost this game, played in November 1983, 1-0.

Action from the same game: John Brogan goes close with McCloy stranded.

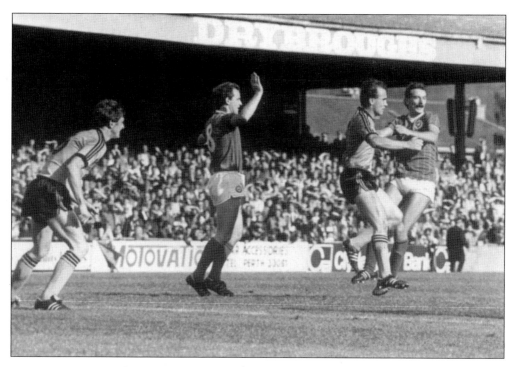

The 1983/84 season again, with John Brogan and Jim Morton taking on Paul Hegarty and Eamonn Bannon at Muirton.

A famous name, albeit at a low ebb in their fortunes: Leeds United visit Muirton for a pre-season friendly on 5 August 1984. Gordon Scott and John Sludden are mounting an attack.

A moment of real tension as Mark Treanor slots home the equaliser from the penalty spot in the famous match against Airdrie on 31 March 1990.

The famous match against Airdrie in March 1990. Roddy Grant rises to power home the goal that would put Saints in the lead for the first time in the game.

The 1991/92 season and a photograph that sums up what all St Johnstone fans expect – with Paul Cherry demonstrating (as Andy Brannigan did in the photograph on page 124) just how to dig in, this time against Celtic.

Being a Saint can be painful. Darren Dods shows a similar commitment to Paul Cherry (above), but with more dramatic results.